EXOTIC
CARS

EXOTIC CARS

Sam Brown

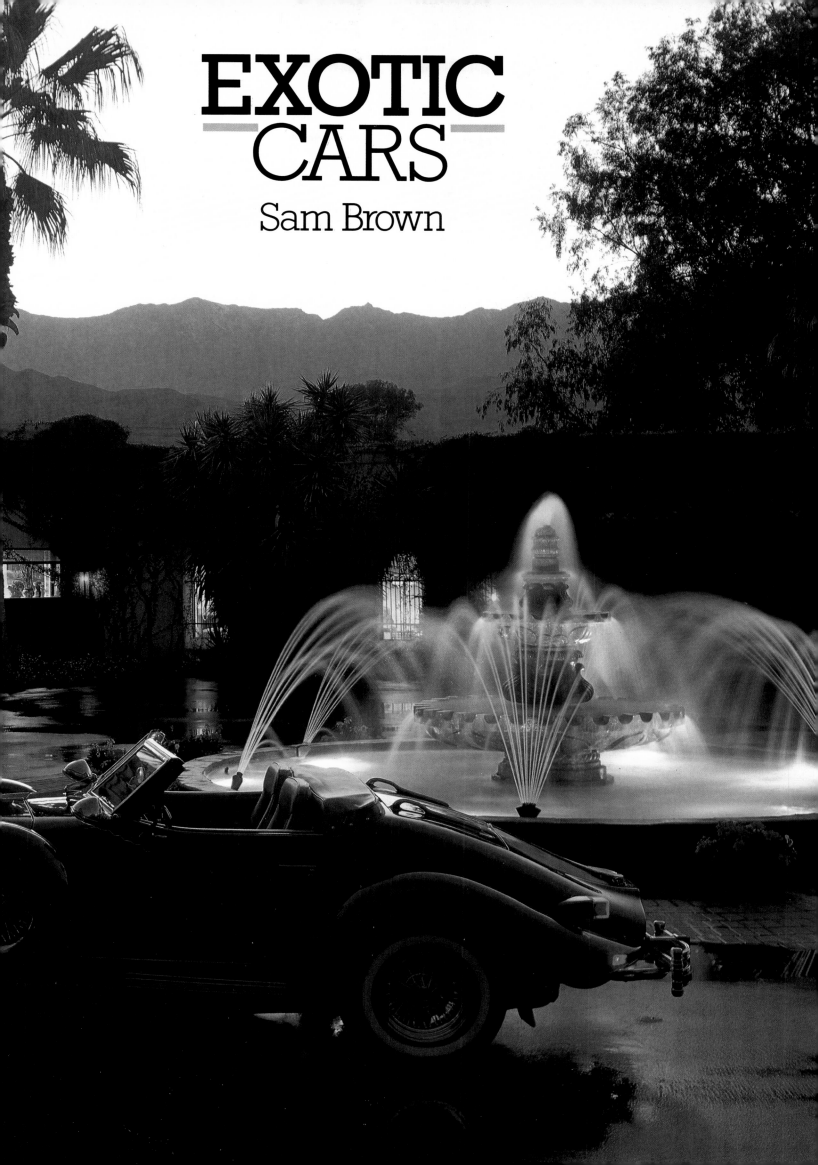

This book was devised and produced by Multimedia Publications
(UK) Ltd

Editor: Jeff Groman
Assistant Editor: Sydney Francis
Design: Millions
Picture Research: Paul Snelgrove
Production: Arnon Orbach, Judy Rasmussen

ISBN 0 8317 3099 4

First published in the United States of America by Gallery Books, an
imprint of W. H. Smith Publishers Inc., 112 Madison Avenue, New
York, NY 10016.

Typeset by The Letterbox Company Ltd
Originated by Imago Publishing Ltd
Printed in Italy by New Interlitho

Below: *High power sports car from TVR — the 390 SE.*
Previous pages: *Hollywood setting for the Excalibur range*

CONTENTS

INTRODUCTION

Over the 100 years or so that the automobile has been in existence, the machine itself has been continually refined and improved to the extent that today even a fairly modest cash outlay buys a fair degree of sophistication in personal transport. But there remains a huge gap between the run of the mill bread-and-butter motor car and the limited edition automobile, the kind of car that if you have to ask the price, you can't afford it.

This book sets out to reveal in words and pictures some of these automobile exotica: a sample from the top of the range of the world's great carmakers – from stately limousines to real red-blooded sports cars – a kind of buyer's guide for those for whom only the best will do.

Superlative luxury: lasting performance

Although this book looks at models current at the time of writing, at this prestige end of the range changes are less frequent and certainly less radical, so that model lines tend to endure rather longer than their stablemates at the more modest end of the sales spectrum.

It is obvious that people who buy cars in this price bracket call for superlative performance to go with the luxury high-level specification. And Italy remains the place to go for truly exotic performance cars, the names Ferrari and Maserati evoking the glamor and excitement of motor racing, while "newcomers" such as Lamborghini continue to produce some of the fastest road cars in the world.

What actually *is* the fastest road car nobody really knows, and until such time as some enterprising organization gets all the contenders – properly prepared – to a suitable high-speed circuit, and puts them against the clock, the great question will never be answered. Of course, there is only a handful of real contenders – and they are all described in this book. One would expect the Ferrari GTO, the Lamborghini Countach and Aston Martin's V8 Vantage to be somewhere in the final reckoning.

Systems excellence

The constant progression of refinement and improvement occasionally sees a sharp leap forward in a particular direction. For instance the application of turbochargers to reasonably small capacity engines can provide very useful performance boosters. The Maserati Biturbo, as its name suggests, goes one further and uses two. In the case of Audi, the company has championed the cause of four-wheel drive.

For many years, all-wheel drive was the prerogative of rugged off-road vehicles used by farmers or adventurers hacking their way through uncharted jungle. On roadgoing cars it has been used with comparative success by Jensen in the Interceptor FF model and by Lotus in Grand Prix racing. But it was in the international rally arena that the system showed its true potential. In loose going, the ability to get as much power as possible down to the road proved an enormous advantage to the Audi team and their Quattros. The original Quattro remains the four-wheel drive "boss car", although the new 200 Turbo provides almost the same degree of high performance and ultimate traction in a spacious saloon body style.

The German carmakers still maintain a high reputation for quality and progressive engineering. Mercedes-Benz recently unveiled their S-Class cars which represent the new top-of-the-range from the Stuttgart-based group. BMW, which tends to have a more overtly sporting image, have moved up-market to challenge Mercedes and the three-pointed star for supremacy. Yet both companies take advantage of the latest technology to make their cars safer – including fitting sophisti-

Below: *Fast car for a fast liver—the James Bond special Lotus Esprit Turbo.* Opposite: *Snow scene for the BMW M635 CSi coupé*

cated equipment such as anti-lock braking which uses a mini computer system to prevent the incautious driver from locking up the road wheels during heavy braking in bad conditions.

Prestige with independence

Britain still boasts the lion's share of the prestige manufacturers. Rolls-Royce remains true to its claim of being "the best car in the world", although even RR has been forced to offer a very slightly down-sized model in the form of the new Silver Spirit and its long wheelbase sister car, the Silver Spur.

Bentley has broken away at last from being a mere Rolls-Royce "clone car" with the arrival of the splendid Mulsanne Turbo model. Which goes some of the way towards restoring the performance image of the famous marque.

Despite the drift towards the creation of larger and larger car conglomerates, many of the small, but highly individualistic, manufacturers continue to exist on very small production runs. Alejandro de Tomaso still sells the output of his small factory, including the expensive and long-in-the-tooth Deauville. An even smaller operation surrounds the exciting Vector with its high-speed potential matched by the fitment of instruments taken from a fighter plane cockpit.

For companies that don't want to merge, there is always the avenue of co-operative ventures. Saab of Sweden and Lancia of Italy have just concluded such an arrangement which produced the new Saab 9000 and the Lancia Thema. Both prestige cars – and definitely exotic – they clearly demonstrate the trend towards making top cars more compact.

USA: where the big car still roams

The greatest area of change has been experienced by the American car industry where the big car has ruled for so long. The risk of fuel shortages forced buyers to try some of the smaller European products, but while their quality of handling and economy was appreciated, the cramped conditions and firm ride made them unattractive for long journeys.

There was also the problem of stifling safety and emission control legislation, which made carmakers fearful of planning anything too advanced in case their schemes were scuppered by new safety rulings. Tough anti-pollution laws required the fitment of special equipment that sapped engine power and turned what should have been a tiger car into a pussycat.

But the Reagan administration decided to go easy on the legislation and give the home industry a stimulus to try something new. The result has been a spate of exciting cars such as the new shape Corvette and Mustang, and aerodynamic shapes for the Ford Thunderbird, Pontiac Firebird and Chevy Camaro. And the famous Cadillac road schooner rolls on.

Perfection's pinnacle

The cars described in this book are more than just status symbols – and certainly more than just a means of getting from one place to another. They represent the pinnacle of perfection, the best on the market, top cars for all tastes and all reasons.

Below: *Still America's own status symbol, the Cadillac Coupé de Ville, but the Rolls-Royce* (right) *is still the ultimate*

ASTON MARTIN LAGONDA

The Aston Martin Lagonda is a truly impressive motor car – the trouble is that it suffers from an identity crisis: sports saloon, straight sports car or luxury saloon?

The car does not sit comfortably in any one niche, but it is certainly striking, extremely comfortable and fast enough for most tastes – the familiar 5.3-liter V8 Aston engine gives the Lagonda a top speed of 143 mph (230 km/h).

With an overall length of 17ft 3in (5.3m), the Lagonda is up among the Rolls-Royces when it comes to taking up parking space. Early models caused a stir with the space age plasma instrument display system.

Interior appointments confirm the pretension to be a luxury saloon, and yet the low-slung design makes it difficult for those who can afford such exotica to get into or out of the car in the dignified manner one might expect of a saloon.

To that end, the Lagonda had been receiving some attention from Aston Martin's specialist coachbuilders, Tickford, who have sought to enhance further the executive appeal.

The latest effort is a long wheelbase version in which an additional 10in of bodywork is grafted into the middle. The extra length is added entirely into the area of legroom, and new and much wider rear doors are fitted with a new roof panel to provide increased headroom.

Included in the price of this conversion (you have to buy a standard car first) are separate air conditioning systems for the front and rear compartments, a stereo system and a rear window blind. Tickford, who specialize in up-market conversions, can also add further custom touches such as on-board television, computers, cocktail bars and radio telephones.

Below: *Lagonda sports saloon. Latest version is stretched to limousine length.*

This page: *The luxury interior with space-age futuristic facia. Under the bonnet, that* magnificent Aston Martin Lagonda engine

ASTON MARTIN V8 VANTAGE

Aston Martin is a hallowed name in British automotive history; a legend enhanced by the taking of some glittering prizes on the race track, including the grueling Le Mans 24 Hours race.

In recent times the company, like many similar institutions, has suffered from the fact that, in a world of mass production and quick cash turnaround, there is not much room to maneuver for a firm making barely four cars a week and using a high level of manual labor to do it.

The controling interest in the company has passed through a number of hands over the past decade, but, thankfully, the Aston Martins still roll slowly out of the workshop at Newport Pagnell. The V8 is produced in three versions – the "ordinary" coupé, the Vantage and the convertible Volante.

To a large extent the car follows the American maxim that there is no substitute for cubic inches. At a time when most car makers are seeking to extract the maximum power from the smallest possible engine, Aston Martin rely on a big, lazy 5.3-liter V8 engine to propel this chunky supercar.

In the "ordinary" V8 the engine develops some 306 bhp, and in the Vantage around 360 bhp. The outputs are slightly vague because Aston tend to adopt the Rolls-Royce attitude when questioned about how much power the engine produces and say simply that output is "sufficient".

In the case of the Vantage it is sufficient to make the model one of the top three fastest road cars in the world with a maximum in excess of 170 mph (273 km/h) and 0 to 60 mph (96.5 km/h) acceleration time of 5.4 seconds.

Unlike many so-called grand touring cars, the Vantage – distinguished by its blanked off radiator grille and deep front spoiler – is as accommodating as it is fast. It will take four people in complete comfort, plus luggage. The 5-speed manual gearbox is standard; automatic is offered on the "ordinary" V8 only.

Below: *A portrait of power—Aston Martin's big muscle car*

AUDI 200 TURBO QUATTRO

Whereas some motor manufacturers prefer to make the charms and potentials of their products as obvious as possible – yards of chromed exhaust pipe, hood power bulges and big fat racing style tires – the Germans tend to go in for understatement.

One would never take the Audi 200 Turbo for a wolf in sheep's clothing, but that is where the mistake is made, because here is a saloon capable of hitting 100 mph (160 km/h) from rest in just a shade over 19 seconds, and going on to a maximum speed of 143 mph (265 km/h) before running out of steam. Add to that the option of 4-wheel drive, and you have a sports saloon that is unique, without any immediate equal or rival.

In one way it represents the current state of the art of carmaking – at least in European terms. Others may offer higher levels of innovative technology, but the Audi range delivers the goods in a practical manner.

The trend towards cars having the drive through the front

wheels produces problems when the power potential reaches a certain point. Too much power at the front can cause a steering "fight" and wheelspin difficulties. The Audi solution has been to offer all its range with 4-wheel drive as a standard option, so that when you want to really take off in a hurry, you can. Spin the turbo up close to the rev limit, slide out the clutch and off you go. No wheelspin, no fuss – and undeniably faster than the 2-wheel drive version.

In keeping with Teutonic tastes the interior is not obviously luxurious, and the instrumentation is somewhat basic when compared with the array of switches and dials, more suited to a space shuttle, that clutter some prestige cars. The only outward concessions to the electronic era include a trip computer, a 10-fault automatic check system and the choice of a really high-tech in-car audio system. The Bosch anti-lock braking system comes as standard.

Above: *A masterpiece of understatement—the 200 Turbo Quattro*

AUDI QUATTRO

This car would be certain to appear in any shortlist of automotive mold-breakers of the decade. It brought 4-wheel drive to a mass-produced road car, and showed that the advantage of putting down the power through *all* the road wheels need not be complex, fragile or horrifyingly expensive.

Add a 2.2-liter, turbocharged 5-cylinder engine to the package and you have a car able to give a good account of itself against more costly and seemingly better-performing rivals.

Audi now offer all-wheel drive across the whole of its range, but those cars are quattros with a small "q": only this car is simply known as the Quattro. It shares the same bodyshell as the coupé, and externally it is hard to spot from the "cooking" car, so is often spared the attention of the highway patrol.

The 200 bhp on tap is barely half the amount of power available to the rally drivers who have put the Audi and the Quattro into a position of dominance in the international rally scene. Others have followed the 4-wheel drive path since, but the Audi Quattro has proved a tough act to follow.

The road car has a top speed of 135 mph (217 km/h) and a 0 to 60 mph (96.5 km/h) time of 7.3 seconds, but if that doesn't do enough to set the adrenalin running, a privileged few buyers will be able to get their hands on the special short wheelbase Quattro.

Only 200 examples of this car have been produced in order for Audi to qualify this an even more potent development car for international competition.

The use of 4-wheel drive in a road car was comparatively rare until the arrival of the Quattro. Its use was mainly for off-road activities in utility vehicles such as Jeeps and Land Rovers, although the British Ferguson company developed a successful 4-wheel drive system for the Jensen sports coupé.

Below: *The car that really started the four wheel drive revolution.*
Overleaf: *in action on the tough Acropolis Rally in 1984*

BENTLEY MULSANNE TURBO

Bentley is one of the most famous names in British motoring history – a fame built largely upon sporting success under the hands of the motor sport giants of yesteryear, such as "Tim" Birkin and his team of muscular machines that challenged the might of the crack Italian teams of Maserati and Alfa Romeo.

Sadly, in more recent times the only difference between the Bentley and its Rolls-Royce stable companion has been the different radiator and the addition of the famous "Flying B" badge, until the emergence of the Mulsanne Turbo – rather more than just a Rolls-Royce with a Bentley badge on it.

The current Bentley range is three strong – the comparatively rare Corniche, the standard Mulsanne (sister to the Rolls-Royce Silver Spirit) and the Mulsanne Turbo. Only the last is sufficiently different to stand on its own as a true Bentley, although the Rolls-Royce parentage is obvious.

For most cars a 6.7-liter engine would be enough, but not when it has to propel almost 2½ tons of motor car. The turbo Bentley has some 100 bhp more than the Rolls-Royce Silver Spirit – double the torque output – which provides a respectable maximum speed of 135 mph (217 km/h), and a 0 to 60 mph (96.5 km/h) time of seven seconds.

Externally, the car shares the same bodyshell as the Silver Spirit, but the Bentley is distinguished by the black painted radiator grille which, say Rolls, is probably worth a few extra miles per hour because it is aerodynamically better than the classic RR slab style grille.

Inside, as befits a car of this quality, luxury is door to door. Top class leather for the electrically adjustable seating, burr walnut panel around the instrumentation, which carries just a discreet "Turbo" badge.

This page: *At last, a high performance Bentley. The Mulsanne is a worthy successor to Bentley sports cars of old, with the luxury touch, including lots of leather and walnut for the interior treatment*

GMB 89X

BITTER SC

Erich Bitter does the most amazing things with Opels, and has been doing so since 1973 when he produced the sleek and exciting CD Coupé, built on the floorpan and drivetrain of the big Opel Diplomat.

Since those days, Bitter has built more cars and now has a big reputation for being able to create machines that are individual, exclusive and exciting, and yet offer levels of reliability and low cost maintenance impossible for most supercar makers.

The SC is the latest of his prestige creations, a device that carries a touch of the Ferrari and Maserati in its classic lines. It has been so successful that Bitter has had to contract assembly and body work out to other plants in Austria and Italy. The standard of finish is very high, the most expensive option with all the trim done in the finest quality leather.

There is a choice of two engines – a 3-liter which provides a maximum speed of 133 mph (214 km/h) and a 3.9-liter specially developed for Bitter, which pushes the SC into the

supercar performer class with a top speed of 142 mph (228 km/h).

While the 2-door SC Coupé provides enough comfort and performance for most, Bitter is aware that his customers, like Oliver Twist, always want more. He has provided it with the new 4-door coupé, which is longer and has a higher roofline than the 2-door, and yet weighs very little more.

A generous 5-seater, the SC 4-door has the same engine options as the 2-door, but Bitter has been working on an even more potent version designed to offer maximum speeds of around 150 mph.

At the other end of the scale, Bitter has just produced an attractive 2-seat Targa-top roadster running on Opel Manta mechanicals. It is called the Rallye – also the name for Bitter's first company – and has a steel body shell protected at each end by integrated plastic fenders. Top speed, using a modified 2.6-liter Opel engine, is claimed to be 138 mph (222km/h).

Above: *The Bitter treatment transforms the mundane into something special*

BMW M635 CSi

This is the latest and most powerful version of the stylish and attractive BMW coupé that still turns heads, despite the fact that its looks are becoming a little dated.

The 'M' prefix gives a clue to the factor that freshens up this particular device – the installation of the powerful 6-cylinder engine designed for the mid-engined M1 coupé with which BMW hoped to challenge the Group 4/5 racing championship.

The M1 is now dead, but that magnificent powerplant lives on in the M635, endowing the car with a 156 mph (251 km/h) maximum speed potential with acceleration to match. In Europe, BMW offer two other variants of the coupé, the 628 and 635 CSi models, but neither possess the performance potential of the M635.

Outwardly there are few indications that this is a wolf in wolf's clothing. It sits slightly lower on wide, fat-tired wheels, and the twin pipe exhaust system might be a giveaway to the knowledgeable few, or to those who do not spot the discreet M-power logo on the front grille and tail panel.

Less obvious concessions to the M635's high performance pretensions include a bigger radiator, beefed up 5-speed manual close-ratio gearbox, limited slip differential and stiffer springing.

As important as it is to get a car like the M635 going as quickly as possible, it is also highly desirable to stop it. The car is fitted with a sophisticated anti-lock braking system developed in conjuction with the Bosch company, which prevents the driver from inadvertently locking the wheels and thus losing road grip and steering ability under emergency braking conditions.

Inside, the car is well set up for two at least. The rear contoured seating is strictly "occasional". Recaro sports seats are standard for front occupants, and the electronic gadgetry includes a trip computer to monitor fuel consumption and journey times, and the ingenious BMW service indicator which lights up a progressive array of lamps to tell the driver how close the car is to its next service.

Spot the difference between the M635 (below) *and the 'ordinary' coupé* (overleaf)

BMW 745i

The microchip is beginning to have a bigger influence on the car – not just by helping to provide information to the driver, but in actually taking certain decisions that may help the car to perform better.

This kind of new technology is recognized, but not always accepted, by some manufacturers who feel that their customers are not yet ready to hand over the driving to a computer. It hasn't quite come to that yet, but BMW clearly believe that their customers are some way down the line with the introduction of the "thinking gearbox" in their top-of-the-range 7-Series car, the 745i.

Since their introduction, the big 7-Series saloons have benefited from a steady program of improvements designed to enhance their appeal as comfortable and roomy sports saloons. Heading the list is the 745i. This has a turbocharged version of the 3.5-liter, 6-cylinder engine, developing some 185 bhp and powering the big car to a maximum 141 mph (228 km/h).

Transmission is via a 4-speed automatic gearbox which has the added bonus that the driver can select any one of three gearchange programs to suit his particular style of driving, including "economy" and "sport" settings. The various factors are fed into a control unit which decides what gear the car should be in at a given moment to get the best performance according to the selected program.

While all this is going on, another set of microchips is beavering away working out the best way to keep the engine running efficiently, and organizing the fuel injection and ignition timing to get the best results. The system also includes a pair of sensors to detect pre-ignition (pinking). This enables the driver to concentrate more on the traffic or relax as much as possible on the journey.

Refinement is a major factor in the latest versions of the BMW 7-Series, and comparatively recent changes to the suspension have enhanced the sporting feel of these big cars, but without spoiling the high level of ride comfort. ABS anti-lock braking is fitted as standard on the 745i.

Below: *Mirror image-solar panel helps to show off the BMW 745i*

BRISTOL BEAUFIGHTER

Bristol Cars has produced less than 3,000 cars since production opened in 1940 during the early years of the last war. After 1945 it became a more significant part of the operation of Bristol Aeroplanes, with the car company running as one of three separate arms of the enterprise.   During 1956, the engine and aeroplane activities were sold to the British Aircraft Corporation and the car business went on its own way. But it has never strayed from its origins and the names of the cars hark back to the famous aeroplanes of the past.

The Beaufighter name was carried by a highly successful twin engined fighter-bomber of World War II. Today it is applied to Bristol's fastest road car, powered by a turbocharged 5.9-liter Chrysler V8 engine.

Bristol modestly decline to quote power outputs or maximum speeds, but there is little doubt that the Beaufighter qualifies easily as one of the fastest supercars around.

The body is basically the established 412 shell but with a Targa removable roof design. It provides ample room for four, plus luggage, and is in every respect a "gentleman's fast tourer".

A convertible version of the Beaufighter is called the Beaufort – yet another name from the aircraft ancestry. The Targa top rollover bar was removed to create the convertible. Early cars were strictly export only, since initial production cars could not comply with British build regulations.

The cost of a Bristol includes that priceless intangible – exclusivity. Current production runs at barely 100 cars a year, all of them lovingly handcrafted by a group of dedicated people.

That is not to say that Bristol is old fashioned or afraid of change. It was the first British carmaker to offer a turbocharged car, and level pegging with Jaguar on first use of disc brakes. Nor is it concerned about buying in expertise. Since 1961 all Bristols have been Chrysler-powered: the engineers chose the American engine even though they had completed a development program on an engine of their own.

Below: *Bristol Beaufighter is the base for the new Beaufort convertible.*

CADILLAC DE VILLE

The process of downsizing was a difficult step for many US car producers, but none more so than Cadillac, the traditional purveyor of those super-long limousines that fill two conventional parking spaces and, fitting the words of the famous Eartha Kitt song, were "long enough to get a bowling alley in the back".

Dropped at the start of the 1986 model year, the large rear-drive De Villes made way for the smaller front-wheel drive Sedan and Coupé De Ville models which were offered with either a 4.1-liter V8 or a 4.3-liter V6 diesel engine.

The overall length of the new De Ville is some 26in less than its rear-wheel drive predecessor, a shortening in length achieved by fitting the V8 engine transversely between the front wheels – the only transversely-fitted V8 offered by any maker in the world. Thus the loss of overall length does not mean a severe cut in the levels of interior space expected by Cadillac customers.

Body design incorporates the use of flush glass for front and rear screens, and the tops of the doors are let into the roofline to allow a hidden drip rail to be incorporated. Coupé De Ville models can have a vinyl roof with "electroluminescent" opera lamps.

The main criterion for the interior is to provide elegant, quiet and spacious accommodation for six people. Leather or cloth trim can be specified and the dashboard is padded from top to bottom with leather-look detailing and simulated butterfly walnut woodgrain.

Instrumentation includes vacuum fluorescent displays for the fuel state, the electronic climate control system and the electronically-tuned stereo. A Fuel Data Center offers information on fuel economy, fuel used and range and there is a telltale warning display about service requirements, indicating what needs attention and when it should be done. Optional extras include a device that automatically dims headlights when other cars are approaching and a three-channel transmitter to operate remote controls for driveway gates and garage doors.

Below: *The "compact" Cadillac, more than two feet shorter than the old car*

CADILLAC ELDORADO BIARRITZ

Just when it seemed that successive energy crises would drive all those big American gas-guzzlers into oblivion, the pressure has eased, fuel costs have stopped escalating wildly, and some Americans are asking for their big cars back.

This is all good news for prestige car makers such as Cadillac where, despite responding to demands for improved fuel consumption, the traditional king-size American car can still be found.

The Eldorado is big and it is expensive, the most expensive version being the Biarritz convertible. This is one of a number of soft top cars appearing after the safety authorities announced that, after all, legislation would not be introduced that would effectively outlaw any convertible.

Besides being costly, the "Eldo" convertible is also heavy. The extra reinforcing required for the body shell in creating a convertible brings the kerb weight to more than two tons, which gives the car's 135 bhp V8 engine a lot of work to do. Transmission is by 3-speed automatic only.

The Eldorado shares its basic body and front wheel drive chassis with the Buick Riviera and the Oldsmobile Toronado. The cars also share the same steering, electrics and self-levelling systems.

Below: *Still a lot of car for the money—Cadillac's "Eldo" Biarritz*

CHEVROLET CAMARO

General Motors is well aware of the need to present a sporting image in order to enhance the appeal of GM products to the new generation of car buyers. Exciting new models such as the Pontiac Fiero and extensive revamps of old stars such as the Corvette all help to spread the message, but to many the real interest lies in the GM muscle car "twins", Pontiac's Firebird and the Chevrolet Camaro – the General's dynamic duo.

Camaro has a special place in US automotive history because it is the car built by GM to challenge Ford's dominance of the ponycar market with the Mustang.

Both cars have benefited from recent reshaping which has made them less bulky, more aerodynamically efficient and certainly more European, inviting comparison with imports such as the German Porsche 944.

"Top dog" car in the Camaro range until recently has been the Z28, the model that went a long way to restoring an otherwise fading performance reputation. This has now been superseded by the IROC-Z Camaro, the car most often featured in IROC races. IROC (International Race of Champions)

is a US motor race series in which the drivers are supposed to compete in cars that are equal, so that driver skill alone is the winning factor. GM capitalize on the race pedigree of the Camaro to produce a road-going version.

Externally the IROC-Z is easily identified by its deep front spoiler and side-skirts – that is if you have already missed those purely cosmetic hood louvers, bright stripes and door panel decals.

In fact, the IROC-Z doesn't need the make-up because it can deliver the performance. The most powerful of the two engines available is the 5-liter V8 with Tuned Port Injection producing 215 bhp, which is mated to a 4-speed automatic transmission. Acceleration from 0 to 60 mph is 6.8 seconds, and a standing quarter mile covered in 15.3 seconds (terminal speed 89 mph – 143 km/h) is good going for a street machine, albeit one with a racing heritage. Beefed up suspension helps drivers to take full advantage of all this power.

Below: *Mean muscle car from GM, Camaro in 1985 trim*

CHEVROLET CORVETTE

Europeans can be a little snooty about American "sports" cars, arguing that sheer straight line performance and interior creature comforts count higher on US scorecards than European demands for good handling and ride qualities.

The Corvette is a splendid example of how the US car industry is emerging from its torpor to produce cars that feature technical innovation and which perform close to standards that would satisfy most European requirements, besides offering plenty of excitement for the home crowd.

In its latest form, the Corvette continues to champion the cause of plastics in car body construction, but it goes a stage further this time with the adoption of plastic suspension springing.

General Motors designed the car to fight on the home showroom floor against fancy imports such as Jaguar, Porsche and Ferrari, and in that respect it does a good job. A 'Vette in European trim was clocked in at a maximum speed of 142 mph (228 km/h) during a test by a respected British magazine, who also obtained a 0 to 60 mph (96.5 km/h) acceleration time of 6.6 seconds – a performance that matches some of the best that Europe can offer.

The power unit is a 5.7-liter V8 engine, uprated for the 1985 models with a "tuned port injection" system designed to increase output by up to 10 per cent. The transmission choice is 4-speed manual with computer operated overdrive, or 4-speed automatic.

New exterior styling is very crisp and clean, and the headlamps retract Porsche-style back into the bonnet when not in use. The Corvette does not pretend to be more than a 2-seater, but the design allows for a fair amount of luggage to be carried by the lucky pair.

Braking improvements for 1985 include the addition of a power booster made, like many other Corvette components, from plastic – the first such installation in an American car.

The driver gets the benefit of an electrically adjustable seat and a really high tech instrument panel which features the best contemporary "solid state" electronics, providing bar graph type displays for engine revs and road speed backed up by more normal digital readouts.

Above and opposite: *New generation Corvette still uses plenty of plastic*

CHRYSLER EXECUTIVE LIMOUSINE

The move towards downsizing popular American cars cannot expect to find approval among the whole range of buyers, many of whom may be reluctant to give up the levels of comfort and interior space they have come to expect in their automobiles.

So it was with Chrysler Corporation's K-Car range, featuring the Le Baron series of crisp modern front-wheel drive cars offering high levels of specification that put them at the top of the mid-size market segment.

But some people want more, and for that reason Chrysler created the Limousine – a car based on the K-Car package that successfully meets demands for extra space and added luxury without sacrificing too much economic performance.

Chrysler build the Limousine on limited volume only. With the jump seats it can seat seven within its 17ft 6in (5.3m) length extended bodyshell which sits on a stretched 10ft 11in (3.4m) wheelbase.

Powerplant is the Japanese Mitsubishi-built 2.6-liter 4-cylinder engine fitted transversely between the front wheels and driving through a Chrysler 3-speed automatic transmission.

High quality standard specification includes an "Ultimate Sound" electronically tuned stereo radio system and plush upholstery in cloth or leather and vinyl.

Other features include a glass divider partition between front and rear with the glass slider power operated, air conditioning, electro luminescent opera lamps, special sound insulation and door to door cut pile carpeting.

This page: *A successful attempt by Chrysler to develop a luxury limousine on their K-Car platform, produced the Executive. Lots of space, legroom and leather*

CHRYSLER FIFTH AVENUE

While car model ranges down at the bottom end of the price list chop and change, grow bigger and smaller and display a wide array of different body shapes and styles, those at the top tend to suffer less from the need to follow fashion, and retain continuity of quality.

This is possibly why the Fifth Avenue has endured so long since its introduction back in 1975. Based on the Dodge Diplomat/Plymouth Grand Fury which is a popular choice with fleet buyers and the police forces, the Fifth Avenue is one of the few remaining V8-powered models in the Chrysler range. For the record, it is also highly regarded in the reliability stakes.

The relatively long production run has meant that the Fifth Avenue has become more and more competitively priced in its market segment where it offers the kind of comfort and style that many American buyers could see disappearing for ever under the pressure of demands for more economical and less ostentatious cars.

Unlike some bidders for the prestige market, the Fifth Avenue has not suffered from the marketing department's insistence that the exterior treatment should include very obvious executive trimmings. Like its smaller-engined, front-wheel drive sister car, the Le Baron-based New Yorker, Chrysler's Fifth Avenue struts its stuff with more subtlety.

The classic large rectangular front grille leads back to a roomy four door saloon body capable of seating six in comfort. The latest version includes a padded landau style roof in vinyl with brushed metal fittings and a choice of cloth or leather for the interior upholstery.

For luxury lovers who may be concerned about saving fuel, the good news is that the latest version of the Fifth Avenue V8 is some eight per cent more economical.

As befits a luxury model, there are power controls for almost everything, including driver seat adjustment, radio aerial and trunk lid; plus cruise control and six speaker in-car stereos.

Below and on following spread: *Traditional American luxury limousine—the Fifth Avenue*

FIFTH AVENUE

41

CITRÖEN CX GTi TURBO

The big Citröen models carry all the quirks and idiosyncrasies that either win friends or make enemies for life. There is no in-between with a Citröen.

The CX bodyshell was introduced as far back as 1974 in order to replace the equally long-running DS model. Both cars were impressive performers in terms of body aerodynamics, but back in those early days such qualities were thought unimportant.

After Citröen's dalliance with Maserati – which produced the striking-looking, very fast but somewhat unreliable Citröen SM – the French firm seemed to abandon any sporting pretensions and concentrated on turning out cars that remained pretty different from the rest, but did little, in performance terms, really to stir the blood.

To be fair, successive energy crises did little to stimulate demand for very quick cars that drank oil and gas like there was no tomorrow, but by the mid-1980s the pressure had eased, and going faster was no longer a problem.

Citröen already had a turbo saloon in the form of the 2500 turbodiesel, but what everybody really wanted was a modern version of the SM without the hassle. It came with the CX GTi – a real supercar saloon capable of speeds up to 136 mph (219 km/h) and with acceleration to match.

The basis for the turbo conversion is the 2.5-liter engine used in the CX GTi, but adding the turbo and other modifications produces a 30 bhp increase in power output.

Despite its fairly heavy weight, the big Citröen is therefore able to give a good account of itself. Apart from the discreet badges, the only significant exterior identification lies in the large rear spoiler set at the base of the deep, curved rear screen. Citröen claim this has the effect of increasing stability and improving the airflow to the extent that the CX GTi Turbo has one of the slipperiest shapes around.

As with other Citröens, the GTi Turbo rides on that unique oleopneumatic suspension which lifts the car like a magic carpet on start-up and subsides with a sigh when the engine is switched off. Unusually, Citröen has turned to conventional instruments for the GTi Turbo, forsaking the curious "cyclop's eye" speedometer for the more usual round dials.

Below: Long-lasting, stylish saloon—now with performance to match the looks

DE TOMASO DEAUVILLE

It was the success of the Jaguar XJ saloons on the Italian market that prompted Alejandro De Tomaso to plan his home-grown competitor; a car that would offer the same levels of luxury and performance as the Jaguar, but which would capitalize on the better reliability of an American Ford V8 engine for the powerplant.

The dimensions and specification of the Deauville matched the Jaguar of the day very closely, but differed in small respects, such as using cloth facings instead of leather upholstery.

The engine has been largely unchanged since the car's introduction. The Ford Cleveland V8 5.7-liter engine, also used in the Pantera, develops 270 bhp. Early cars had a still more powerful version.

The Deauville is a very conservative car – a less kind description would be "old-fashioned". Changes over the years have been few, and include the fitment of vents behind the front wheel arches to release heat from the engine compart-

ment. Air conditioning, power-assisted brakes, electric windows and a fully upholstered trunk space are part of the standard specification for the Deauville.

Production levels are small, possibly smaller than 50, and a high proportion of the cars go to export markets all over the world.

Unfortunately for De Tomaso, one of the best potential markets – the USA – is closed to the Deauville. The car does not meet US emission control or safety requirements, and for the production volume concerned De Tomaso feels it would not be worth adapting the car for this market.

Meanwhile the Deauville continues to sell well in Italy, being bought by well-heeled customers who enjoy its exclusivity. Another important factor in selling to this sector of Italian society is that the car adapts well to armor plating!

Below and right: Italy's answer to the Jaguar, De Tomaso's Deauville

EXCALIBUR

The Excalibur is the kind of car that must have been built with Hollywood in mind – the company that makes them describes these big 1930s-style roadsters as "a triumph of function and style". Function may be rather understated, but no one could deny that the cars have style.

It all began back in 1964 when the Stevens brothers were working on the idea of producing a car based on the design of the 1927 Mercedes-Benz, but using modern Studebaker Avanti components.

The idea was to use the car as a show-stopper for Studebaker at the New York motor show of 1964. Unfortunately, Studebaker chose that moment to decide it was going to quit the car business, so the two Stevens brothers Steve and David, and their father Brooks, decided to go it alone. The show debut of this impressive car was a smash hit.

Since then, Excalibur has produced more than 3,000 vehicles, the latest version being the Series IV Phaeton, with its enormous 10ft 5in (3.6m) wheelbase and very high level specification.

The power unit is a GM V8 of 305 cubic inches with a 4-speed automatic gearbox. Standard equipment on the car incudes electrically adjustable seats that have a range of six different movements.

Other luxury touches include leather-trimmed seats, cruise control, dual air horns, burled walnut dashboard and a spectacular paint job to go with that long bonnet, huge exhaust outlets, and the dramatic sweeping lines of the bodywork.

It is certainly a car for the stars. Famous names such as Tony Curtis, Dean Martin, Sonny and Cher and Shirley Jones have owned them, but Phyllis Diller must be the biggest of the Excalibur fans: she has bought four.

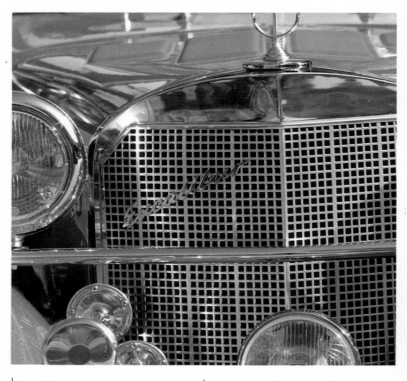

This page and following spread: *Amazing Thirties styling with modern mechanicals—Excalibur grabs the attention*

FERRARI TESTAROSSA

Perhaps not the fastest, and certainly not the prettiest, product from Modena, the Testarossa is certainly one of the most dramatic machines born out of the union between Ferrari engineering expertise and the styling flair of Pininfarina.

Testarossa (meaning "red head") revives a famous name from Ferrari motor racing history when the engine that powered the highly successful sports and racing car of 1958 carried red painted cam covers.

The new Testarossa also is capable of a performance that would not look too out of place on a race track: a maximum speed of more than 180 mph (290 km/h) and acceleration from 0 to 62 mph (100 kp/h) in 5.8 seconds.

Like its famous namesake, the new Ferrari has red cam covers on the flat-12 "boxer" engine which, in this installation, develops a claimed 390 bhp. Only the limited production GTO is faster among Ferrari's stable of thoroughbreds.

Designed as a replacement for the BB 512, the Testarossa is low, handsome and very, very wide. Across the beam, the car measures 77.8 in (197.6 cm). The reason for this has nothing to do with the Italian *penchant* for a shapely and substantial *derrière*, but is an engineering decision to move the radiators cooling the mid-mounted engine from the front of the car to the middle. Hence the deep ribbed channels in the doors to channel air into the ducts for the radiators.

The move allowed Pininfarina to produce a lower and more aerodynamic front and to provide a little more luggage space in the front compartment which supplements the meagre stowage at the rear. Even so, there is barely room for even a pair of slimline Gucci bags. It is likely that anyone who can afford the price tag will not be too concerned about maintenance costs, but it might be comforting for them to know that the engine/transmission system is mounted on a separate chassis subframe that can be detached for easy access.

Above and opposite: *The latest from Ferrari—the return of the "Red Head" Testarossa*

FERRARI GTO

The year 1984 must go down as a vintage one in the diary of any Ferrari enthusiast because two new cars were announced from Modena, and one of them was a new GTO.

There was a decent enough interval between the debut of the GTO at the Geneva Show and the Testarossa later in the year at Paris, but striking though the new "redhead" may be, it must stand in the shadow of the GTO "boss" car, claimed to be the world's fastest production car, with a maximum speed of 184 mph (296 km/h).

The first GTO, the 250 announced in 1962, is now worth a fortune on the collector's market. Only 44 of these original cars were built – the required number at the time to allow the car to be raced as a "production" machine.

Now, 23 years later, it takes 200 factory-produced GTOs plus some 15 "development" cars to allow the new version to race under international Group B regulations.

The 308 ancestry is obvious in the 1984 GTO, although it has a longer wheelbase, and the Pininfarina design retains the deep side scoops feeding air to the twin turbocharged engine set fore and aft, straddling the center line of the car.

While the original GTO had a V12 engine under the bonnet, the latest version has a V8. This is derived from the 308 unit, but has slightly reduced capacity so that in turbo form it is equivalent to a 4-liter non turbo-charged engine.

The lucky 200 who get to buy the cars can be almost certain that they own the fastest current production car in the world. Trying hard, the GTO gets up to 62 mph (100 km/h) in 4.9 seconds, flashes past the quarter mile in 12.7 seconds traveling at 124 mph (199 km/h), and goes on to reach speeds approaching 200 mph (322 km/h) flat out.

Below and following spread: *Possibly the fastest production road car in the world—the exclusive Ferrari GTO*

FIAT X1/9

The "pocket Ferrari" is how many enthusiasts would describe Fiat's small and attractive mid-engined sports car. This first appeared at a time when most manufacturers were turning away from sports cars and into other more mundane – but also more lucrative – areas of car making.

In early examples, the smaller 1300cc engine was laid transversely behind the seats, resulting in a less than sparkling performance that did not really allow the spirited driver to take advantage of the very good handling and maneuverability of the little car.

The stylish wedge-shaped bodyshell with its Targa top was designed by Bertone, who have now taken over production of the X1/9, but only in its latest form as the VS "Verzione Speziale". For some time now it has been fitted with the Fiat 1500cc engine used in the Strada/Ritmo series, and a 5-speed gearbox, which allows the car to reach 106 mph (170 km/h) maximum speed.

Strictly a 2-seater, the X1/9 has two luggage compartments – the usual practise forced by a mid-engine configuration. The compartment at the front is of little use if the Targa top is stowed, and the slimline section at the back, close to the engine, is no place to stow the groceries!

The basic style is unchanged since the car appeared during the early 1970s, apart from the addition of extended bumpers. It remains a bargain price admission to the special world of the Italian sports car and it is a tribute to the original design that the Fiat X1/9 remains as popular as ever.

The most recent claim to fame of the little car was as a mobile test for the ill-fated De Lorean stainless steel sports car. Assessing the possibility of a Ford V6 as a potential powerplant, the big engine was shoehorned into the Fiat to see how it worked in a transverse installation. The result was said to be "fun to drive", and the Red Rocket, as it was called, provided plenty of fun, until the experimental driveline cried, "enough!" and literally blew into pieces all over the road.

This spread: *Fiat's "pocket Ferrari", the X1/9 now built by Bertone*

FORD CONTINENTAL MARK VII

Ford stated its intent to take a serious interest in car aerodynamics at the New York Auto Show of 1982 when it showed the rounded streamlined shape of the Continental Concept 90 cars. That theme has been passed on since then to the top line of US Ford's image cars, the Thunderbird and Mercury Cougar, and to the elegant luxury touring coupé, the Continental.

The performance version of the Mark VII is the LSC Series powered by a special 5-liter fuel-injected V8 engine, and the suspension is stiffened to take the extra surge available.

The radical change wrought upon the Continental is not restricted to its exterior; in many ways it has become a rolling showcase for some of Ford's most sophisticated electronics systems that make driving safer, easier and very much more luxurious. For example, all models feature an electronically-controlled air suspension system that provides self-leveling, plus an improvement in ride and handling that puts the big car close to European standards.

An important safety feature on the car is the fitment of an electronically controlled 4-wheel anti-skid system which uses its own computer to monitor the wheel rotation rates and balance braking effort to prevent wheel lock-up.

Ford designers have really responded to the electronic revolution with the Continental's impressive array of microchip technology. There are digital readouts for speed, distance and fuel contents and electronically-controlled monitoring of the push-button in-car climate system.

There is no need to sweat too much about getting the seat adjustment right either, for the LSC's sports seats have a six-way electric adjustment system, although the thigh support has to be worked by hand!

Extra cost options include a keyless entry system using an individual code tapped out on a door-mounted keypad, mobile telephone and a device that allows the driver to open his garage door without getting out of the car.

Below and right: Streamlining and lots of electronics for the latest Continental

FORD MUSTANG

The Mustang, for so long the star of the "pony car" class, is the car that almost lost its way.

In the halcyon winning days of the Boss 302 Trans-Am during the late 1960s and early 1970s the Mustang could almost do no wrong, but successive revisions by Ford made it heavier, and with the Mustang II lost any remaining pretension to being regarded as a muscle car.

In its latest form, which arrived in 1979, the balance was redressed somewhat but the sparkle was still missing. Attempts to add a turbo produced a car that made more noise but failed to deliver on the speedometer, and it was only when Ford decided to offer the option of a 5-liter V8 engine in the pretty bodyshell that the Mustang looked ready to gallop back to the top of the poll.

However, it took a little bit of European influence to produce a real muscle Mustang in the form of the machine devised by the Ford Special Vehicle Operations.

Inspired by the success of the German Zakspeed Capris with their small capacity tuned and turboed engines, Ford SVO took the same route with the Mustang. The basic powerplant is the 2.3-liter fuel injection turbocharged four already used in the Thunderbird and Cougar but with a few extra tweaks collected from race experience. The result is a maximum speed of up to 130 mph (209 km/h) and 0 to 60 mph (96.5 km/h) in about 7 seconds.

It also means that Ford is once again up in the vanguard of US performance cars, which is important from a marketing standpoint when, after years of being foisted off with dreary "econoboxes", the American car buyer has rediscovered the great love affair with the motor car and had the desire for speed and performance rekindled.

External modifications to the SVO are kept to a minimum. The most significant difference between this and the standard car is the revised frontal treatment, together with the hood air scoop for the turbo intercooler and the biplane rear wings.

Above and left: *Special high performance version of the new look Mustang—thanks to Ford SVO*

FORD THUNDERBIRD TURBO

The latest shape for this classic American car has been described as one of the most radical redesigns to emerge from Detroit in the past quarter century.

Perhaps that description is a little over the top, but there is no doubt that the appearance of the smooth and rounded aerodynamic T-Bird rekindled an interest in Ford's sporting supercar that had fallen progressively out of favor with the enthusiast owner.

At first the new Thunderbird and its Mercury sister car, the Cougar, were only available with the Ford 3.8-liter V6 engine. This was followed shortly afterwards by the offer of a 5-liter fuel-injected V8. Both engines were matched with automatic transmission.

The one everyone was waiting for, however, was the Turbo. This would add the final touch to the T-Bird's return to enthusiast approbation and, secondly, it would repair some of the image damage done by Ford's earlier and disastrous attempt to add turbo power to the 2.3-liter engine in the Mustang.

By clever application of the latest electronics techniques, Ford sorted out the problem of fuel injection. Revised piping and other modifications also helped to smooth out performance and help the engine to deliver the goods. A 5-speed manual gearbox is standard on the Turbo.

The modifications have not been restricted to the power plant. Ford has made a big effort to give the T-Bird Turbo a ride and handling to match the engine by fitting a new Quadra-Shock rear suspension system to smooth out power delivery to the driven back wheels.

The Turbo is expected to account for only a small proportion of T-Bird sales: not enough for Ford to go overboard on distinguishing the model. Externally, there is only discreet badging plus a slightly styled nose carrying underslung spotlights to indicate the turbo potential. Inside there are "articulated" seats and special high level electronic instrumentation, which includes warning lights for over-boost.

Below: *Turbo power give the T-Bird a performance boost. Facia (right) features high-tech display*

JAGUAR XJ-S HE

Since the days of the SS, the C-type and D-type racers and, more recently, the lean and mean looking E-type, the name of Jaguar has held a special magic and a very special place in the world of the sports car. Current carrier of the scepter for Jaguar is the XJ-S which, although launched back in 1975, is still able to challenge and see off younger upstart rivals.

The XJ-S is offered with a choice of powerplants – the 5.3-liter V12 and, the newly-developed AJ6 3.6-liter 6-cylinder unit designed for the new XJ40 saloon.

In essence, this means that the XJ-S will be the last Jaguar to carry the famous V12 engine under its long sleek bonnet. In its latest form the V12 has been worked on by Swiss engineer Michael May – or at least Jaguar has adopted May's novel "Fireball" combustion chamber principle in an effort to make the fuel consumption more reasonable – hence the HE (High Efficiency) tag.

The styling of the XJ-S is somewhat controversial and not to every taste. That long bonnet is redolent of the sports cars of old, but the chief complaint is reserved for the rear quarters with the small upright rear window set between steel flying buttresses.

The rear view is the one that most road users are likely to see most frequently as the XJ-S sweeps swiftly up towards its maximum speed of 153 mph (246 km/h), reaching 60 mph (96.5 km/h) in 5.6 seconds. But it is not just the fact that the car achieves such a performance, it is *how* it does it. The sheer refinement of the machine is something that rivals such as Mercedes and BMW have been trying to match for years.

The 3-speed automatic gearbox is standard fit on the V12, although a 5-speed manual is offered on the smaller 3.6-liter car. The ride is soft – perhaps a shade too soft for a sporting car – but it performs as a splendid grand tourer; although strictly for two passengers over long journeys, as rear seat legroom is very cramped despite the large overall dimensions.

Below: *Fast cat. V12 power makes the XJ-S a supercar performer in the Jaguar tradition*

JAGUAR XJ SOVEREIGN

It is seldom that a manufacturer is encouraged to hold back the introduction of a new model because the current design is selling so well, but that is just what happened to Jaguar in the case of the XJ saloons and the new XJ40 waiting in the wings.

That the XJ series should still be in such demand after a production run of more than 16 years is a tribute to the original design for a saloon that truly meets the old Jaguar maxim of grace, pace and space and which has remained fresh and attractive over all those years.

Many other European manufacturers with more modern machines in their showrooms must find it galling that a 16-year-old design remains the benchmark against which their latest products of high-tech will be judged.

There are four XJ saloons in the latest range, the top two both designated with the Sovereign nomenclature taken from Daimler and available with a choice of the 4.2-liter XJ 6-cylinder engine or the 5.3-liter V12 HE. (The latter is available with automatic transmission only.)

Anyone who has ridden in or driven one of the big Jaguars will appreciate what a hard act they are to follow. It is easy to see why so many of these roomy and comfortable cars wind up as flagships of many company fleets, although they are not stately chauffeur-driven devices. Despite the heavyweight body, the big Jaguars turn in quite a potent performance, offering a maximum speed in excess of 130 mph (209 km/h), plus lively acceleration.

It is sad to reflect that once the present XJ saloons have gone, that magnificent V12 engine will be available only in the XJ-S sports car. The new Jaguar saloon, which is planned to be lighter and with much better aerodynamic performance, will have the smaller but more economical AJ6 3.6-liter, 6-cylinder engine already in a coupé and cabriolet version of the XJ-S.

Left: *Luxury with performance—the Jaguar XJ Sovereign. Interior is to a high specification*

LAMBORGHINI COUNTACH

Understatement is a word with which the people at Lamborghini are not familiar, but to call the Lamborghini Countach "striking" would be such an understatement.

The Bertone design, first shown as far back as 1971 at the Geneva Show, fairly shrieks "supercar", and that is even before you have seen those amazing forward-hinging doors, or experienced the raw power of the V12 engine that drives this incredible machine up to a maximum speed of close to 170 mph (273 km/h), and reaches 60 mph (96.5 km/h) in a shattering 5.6 seconds.

In its latest form, the LP 500S has a 4.7-liter version of the original 3.9-liter V12 engine, producing around 375 bhp. Every engine undergoes two days of testing at the Sant' Agata factory in Italy, before being slotted into the middle of the amazing bodyshell, which is knee high, but as wide as a Rolls-Royce Phantom limousine.

That width helps to make the car immensely stable on its big tires – which are smaller at the front – and the near to perfect balance possible with a mid-engine configuration makes the Countach a car than can hurtle around corners with confidence.

It is certainly no town car. Apart from the width of the shapely bodywork, driver visibility is not of the best – especially to the rear – but then there are not too many things capable of overtaking the Countach.

Extra stability at speed can be had with the addition of a rear wing, such as those fitted to Formula One racing cars, but it does reduce overall top speed slightly because of the increased drag.

Compared to other supercars such as the Ferrari BB 512 which has a similar design configuration, the Countach is quite compact. In the Bertone design this has been achieved by keeping the cabin area well forward between the front wheels. The catch has been the need to increase the width to get space for the feet.

Below and left: The car that stands out in the crowd—Lamborghini's striking Countach. Lean, mean and very, very fast

LANCIA THEMA

In recent times the fortunes of the famous Lancia company have been in decline. All its history and heritage could not protect Lancia from the loss of public confidence following the corrosion problems with the Beta series. But, while some of the coupé models were selling well, Lancia was missing out at the executive end of the scale, where the stylish but aging Gamma was not quite able to carry the flagship banner.

Helped by the giant Fiat organisation Lancia turned to an international cooperation project with the prestigious Swedish carmakers Saab (where the management was also looking to build a top-of-the-range model) to try to find a replacement.

The ideal would have been a common car, but it didn't work out that way. Quite early on it was apparent that the two different markets required different cars, and so the projects began to diverge. In the end Saab got the 9000 and Lancia the Thema, the only common components being a dozen minor pressings in the engine compartment.

But for all that divergence, there is a similarity between them, although the Lancia is clearly and deliberately more conservative, aiming at subtle style and understated prestige instead of studied high tech, fancy instrumentation and gimmicks. Curiously, the Fiat car developed on the back of the Thema project does go for the ultra-modern presentation, more streamlined shape and electronic gadgetry more characteristic of the Saab.

There are a number of versions of the Lancia Thema to be made available with four engine options including a 2-liter turbocharged petrol engine and a turbo diesel.

The version that may be worth waiting for involves input from another area of the vast Fiat empire – Ferrari. The plan is to sell some of those famous engines to use in other cars, and one prospect in the Thema. The engine would, however, be too powerful even in detuned form, so Lancia is examining the possibility of making this supercar 4-wheel drive as well.

Below: The Thema is Lancia's new flagship for the model range

LOTUS ESPRIT TURBO

If the chassis building expertise and engine development experience of a Grand Prix car constructor is mixed with the design flair of one of Italy's most talented designers, the result is a recipe for a world-beater.

All these ingredients were present to make the Lotus Esprit Turbo the fastest and most expensive model in current production from that famous Lotus factory deep in the Norfolk countryside. The Turbo shares the same 2.2-liter engine as the "ordinary" Esprit as well as the mid-engined wedge-shaped body package designed by Giorgetto Giugiaro of ItalDesign. Good though it is, the normally aspirated Esprit is a little left out in the performance stakes against rivals such as Lamborghini and Ferrari. Hence the addition of the turbo, which helps the car to achieve a maximum speed of nearly 150mph (241 km/h) with acceleration to match.

The decision to locate the engine in the middle of the chassis was made simply to provide an almost perfect weight distribution arrangement, so vital in seeking ultimate handling performance.

Through its founder, the late Colin Chapman, Lotus established a worthy reputation for making cars which went round corners faster than anything else, and the Esprit Turbo continues that tradition with leech-like roadholding.

The engine installation itself is worthy of closer study because, unlike so many turbocharger applications where the device is bolted on with the aim of getting as much power as possible, Lotus took a more subtle approach.

One of the major bugs in many turbo installations is the creation of a lag while the exhaust-driven turbocharger spins up towards full boost, with the result that maximum power cannot be available on small throttle openings.

Without resorting to high-tech solutions, Lotus engineers have designed a system that provides a high degree of engine flexibility and plenty of low down punch. Lotus have come up with a Turbo Esprit that can play pussycat as easily as it can play tiger.

Above: *Fast mover the Turbo Esprit. Cabin* (left) *is snug*

MASERATI BITURBO

After the charisma-packed and very obvious supercar productions such as the Merak and the Kyalami, the Biturbo must have seemed something of a disappointment to fans of the Maserati marque.

It was in fact a very real attempt to produce a Maserati for the masses at a time when the supercars were under threat, and Maserati itself, under the ownership of Alessandro de Tomaso, was feeling the pinch.

The answer was thought to be in producing something approaching a volume car – the kind of thing that could compete in both price and performance against mid-range prestige cars from Germany, such as the BMW 528 injection.

The bodyshell has an attractive two door configuration, featuring a typical Maserati front grille distinguished by the famous trident motif. As its name suggests, the V6 engine of the Biturbo has its power output boosted by the addition of twin turbochargers. On the Italian market, where the taxation system limits capacity, the engine is only a 2-liter, but other markets get the 2.5-litre V6, developing some 200 bhp and endowing the car with a 130 mph (209 km/h) top speed potential.

Although mass appeal is the stated objective, the Biturbo makes few obvious concessions to the world of mass production. You will find no acres of plastic here, but a closer look reveals that what appears to be leather on the seats is not, and the instrumentation is borrowed from the more mundane Lancia Delta.

With any Maserati, however, it is the performance of the car that really matters, and in that respect the 2.5-liter Biturbo is no disappointment. An Italian expects a performance car to sound like one, and in this respect the Biturbo should please all those budding race stars who compete in impromptu grand prix around the streets of Turin and Milan.

Plans to extend the appeal of the car further include a longer wheelbase, 4-door version called the 425 which was shown in prototype form at the Frankfurt Show of 1983.

Originally planned as the "Maserati for the masses", the Biturbo has helped to move this famous Italian carmaker a little closer towards volume production. Latest version is a convertible

MERCEDES-BENZ 500SEC

This is the biggest, most expensive and possibly the most attractive Mercedes-Benz you could buy. Flagship of the S-Class range, the 500SEC has clean and elegant lines that disguise its bulk.

It would be easy to think that the SEC is merely a two door, lowered-roof version of its saloon sister, but this is not so. The coupé differs quite substantially with a shorter wheelbase and overall length, but wider and lower than the saloon.

Like the others of its class, the SEC is built to the much vaunted Mercedes "energy concept" in which its engineers have tried to make significant gains in economy without a noticeable effect on overall performance. In the case of the coupé the job of the engine is eased a little by the decision to cut down on body weight by using aluminum instead of steel for the hood, trunk lid and rear bulkhead.

The model was still under development when the car industry woke up to the advantages of good aerodynamic performance for body designs. It fitted well with the current energy concepts, and the designers were able to create a shape with a commendably low drag factor of 0.34 (0.36 for the saloon), so that the all-alloy V8 engine has less work to do and is more economical.

One obvious concession to smoothing the air flow can be seen in the neat way that the windscreen wipers tuck down behind the lip of the hood.

Unlike many coupés, the SEC is capable of seating four in comfort. The high level standard specification includes special contoured seats with electrically operated adjustment, and cruise control so that motorway speeds can be set and maintained without throttle pedal pressure.

A clever detail touch – if a little unnerving to new passengers – is the seat belt system. As soon as the engine is started, a special arm extends over the shoulder of the occupant, "offering" the seat belt buckle. Once the harness has been fixed, the arm retracts out of the way.

Mercedes needed to work out a solution like this because the coupé body lacks a center pillar upon which to fix a conventional belt arrangement. They say, however, that the "robot belt server" is a better encouragement to belt up and stay safe than any warning buzzer or flashing light.

Right: *Big car classic. New S-class has smooth rounded lines*

MITSUBISHI STARION

Having built up a reputation for producing well-equipped and reliable, albeit rather dull, motor cars, the Japanese car-makers have moved into the next stage of their development by turning towards more overtly sporty products to head up their ranges.

Nissan has already proved it can be done with the highly successful Z-cars, and Toyota shapes up nicely with cars like the Celica Supra. Mitsubishi's sporting challenge is carried by the Starion: a meaty-looking 2 + 2 coupé that is already giving a good account of itself in European motor sport competition.

The style is strictly European: crisp and clean, slightly angular, and with a low slung purposeful look that makes it stand out as a performance car. It delivers, too. The 2-liter turbocharged engine, which comes from the Lancer 2000 Turbo, propels the Starion to a maximum speed of 133 mph (214 km/h) and from 0 to 60 mph (96.5 km/h) in 7.5 seconds.

Aware that owners are likely to want to enjoy the Starion's vivid performance to the full, the suspension package has been designed to provide handling to match its power – but at the expense of a rather harsh ride. However, the engine is wonderfully smooth, helped by the special balancer shafts running inside which damp out the vibration problems usually experienced with bigger capacity 2-liter engines.

Pop-up headlamps and an integral front bumper aid the aerodynamics, and one clever feature of the body design is the way in which the safety belt system has been built into the doors. This avoids the risk of passengers tripping over belts or reel boxes as they climb into the rear seats of the car. The catch is that the doors, which have two latches, are very heavy.

While billed as a 2 + 2, the Starion is essentially a 2-seater. Rear room is at a premium and there is no space for luggage at all unless the rear seats can be folded down and used as an extension of the cargo space.

Below: *Japanese muscle car — the Starion Turbo. Interior* (right) *has only occasional-use rear seats*

PANTHER SOLO

The exciting mid-engined Panther Solo sports car was not really expected to progress much farther than just a concept, an image booster for the small British-based company while a real production model was prepared to succeed the traditional Kallista 2-seater.

The style of the Kallista has its roots back in the 1930s, whereas the Solo is very much a car of the 1980s, and is a clever compromise between something that is *avant garde* but also a practical production possibility. Design is all-British, with the chassis produced by Len Bailey, who also crafted the famous Ford GT40 chassis.

In the low-slung, short-nose design, driver and passenger sit well forward between the wheels in the fashionable Group C racer style. The rest of the aluminum body sweeps back past the wide rear quarters which carry the cooling ducts for the transverse mid-engine.

Early models had a Ford 1.6-liter CVH engine and drive train taken straight from the European Ford Escort XR3i. Other powerplants considered for the Solo included the Peugeot 205 Turbo 16, but Panther would need to advance its plans to make a future Solo with all-wheel drive to take this engine.

The present owner of the Panther company, Young C. Kim, is well aware of the need for production economies. For example, the chassis and body pressings for the Kallista are done in one of Kim's plants in Korea and shipped to Britain for the assembly process. Solo major components are to be made in Britain, but the car will feature a number of items borrowed from the Ford parts bin for Escort and Sierra models.

There are obvious advantages in borrowing parts, and Panther has successfully followed this route before, although a design as specialised as the Solo does mean that some components, for instance the front brakes, need to be modified.

In performance terms, the Solo should be well able to hold its own. The "standard" 1.6-liter car has a claimed maximum of 120 mph (193 km/h) and a 0 to 60 mph time of 7.9 seconds. Under development is a 1.6-liter turbo-powered car with a further 10 mph on top speed and 0 to 60 mph in 7.1 seconds. Bailey is also looking at the 2.3-liter US Ford engine with turbo, but that would need 4-wheel drive to handle the 180 bhp it produces.

Below: *Panther's new sports car could have a career in racing*

PININFARINA SPIDEREUROPA

There are some designs that just will not lie down and die, either because the manufacturer introduces a steady program of improvements to keep them fresh, or because the basic concept has a universal and long-lasting appeal.

The latter case is certainly true with the Pininfarina Spidereuropa. Essentially the Fiat 124 Sport of the 1960s, the giant Italian carmaker found its small volume production did not fit with their plans, and so Pininfarina took it on, enhanced it and kept it going.

The fortunes of the Spidereuropa have seen a boost from the fact that American proposals for new car safety regulations were anti-convertibles, and many carmakers fought shy of designing any more "ragtops". The regulations were subsequently scrapped, but not until there were so few convertibles around that the Spidereuropa was in demand.

It remains a truly classic 2-seater Italian sports car, clean and uncluttered and yet with a slight vintage feel that must appeal to the growing number of people looking for a car to restate the old values and stand out from the crowd.

The engine is a 2-liter, 4-cylinder Fiat unit developing 105 bhp and driving through a 5-speed manual gearbox. Maximum speed is around 111 mph (180 km/h) and it accelerates from 0 to 60 mph (96.5 km/h) in just under 10 seconds.

This may not be an earth-shattering performance, but that sporting crackle from the exhaust and the wind in the hair when the excellent folding hood is down guarantee the return of at least some of the exhilaration that is missing from modern motoring.

Left: *Refined through the years, the Spidereuropa is as attractive as ever*

Above, left and following spread: *Big "whale tail" spoiler distinguishes the ultimate 911 Porsche*

PORSCHE 911 TURBO

This is what the *afficionados* call a "proper Porsche" because it has the engine at the back. Detractors – usually people who are unable to afford one – refer to them as "just very fast Volkswagens".

There is, of course, the link between these two very different cars: in Dr Porsche they share the same designer. Both have the engine at the back, but there the similarity ceases.

The 3.3-liter 911 Turbo is without doubt the superstar of the Porsche range, although it is no secret that the original plan by the Stuttgart concern had been to phase out the rear-engined car in favor of the new, more conventional front-engine models, starting with the 928.

But the 911 just wouldn't lie down, and the car got a new lease of life when it was decided to turbocharge the flat 6-cylinder air-cooled engine to produce a performance so searing that the 911 now ranks among the world's top five fastest road cars. Maximum speed is in excess of 160 mph (257 km/h), and it can reach 60 mph (96.5km/h) in a heart-stopping 5.1 seconds – and all this with only a 4-speed gearbox.

Some of the attraction towards this car must come from the fact that to even get close to enjoying the full performance potential you really have to know what you are doing. The 911 is no car for beginners or road hogs who lack the skill.

Not that it is inherently dangerous – far from it – simply that the arrangement of the engine at the back, hanging out beyond the rear axle, creates an interesting distribution of weight which can cause the car to bite back in certain circumstances if the power or steering are crudely applied. Ownership therefore speaks as much about the ability to drive as it does about the ability to find the money to buy the car.

The 911 is certainly an eye catcher with that big "whale tail" rear spoiler and extended wheel arches to accommodate the wide section wheels and tires, and it is certain that Porsche foresee many more years of life for this really red-blooded machine.

PORSCHE 928S

The 928 was the second front-engined sports car to come from Porsche in its unsuccessful attempt to break away from the rear engine tradition that had served it for so long.

First came the 924, the Stuttgart boy racer machine built around Audi mechanics, which failed to meet its promise of providing a Porsche at a price everyone could afford.

The second car was pure Porsche, and although the configuration was the same as the 924, this bigger sister broke a lot of new ground in its concept, to the extent that the 928 earned itself the coveted European Car of the Year award.

It is a big car but, although roomy for two, the handsome bodyshell offers only cramped, occasional accommodation for any more, which is a pity because as a long distance mile-eater the 928 comes pretty close to the top of the tree. The first models with the brand new 4.7-liter V8 engine began to meet the performance promise and, subsequently, the boosting of the power output for the Series 2 cars up to 310 bhp pushed the 928 firmly into the Supercar category.

Maximum speed is in excess of 150 mph (241 km/h), and acceleration from 0 to 60 mph (96.5 km/h) is achieved in 6.7 seconds – fast enough to leave the rest of the field gasping at the lights.

The styling has remained remarkably fresh – a tribute to the original concept – and while it might lack the charisma of its potent rear-engined stablemate the 911, it scores highly as a true performance car.

In terms of handling the 928 benefits from excellent balance and weight distribution, aided by the fact that, as with the 924, the gearbox sits down at the back of the car, being installed as a unit with the rear axle and final drive.

Below: *Striking design for the big, front-engined Porsche. Interior* (bottom) *befits a performance car*

RENAULT TURBO 2

The Renault Turbo 2 is essentially a Renault 5 and, despite the "squashed frog" look created by those enormous wheelarch extensions, the shape of Le Car is still lurking in there somewhere.

Turbo 2 is in fact a version of the original Turbo 1 model designed for the production line, and to comply with Homologation requirements for racing. The power unit is Renault's 1400cc 4-cylinder engine, fitted with Bosch fuel injection and capped with a turbocharger, which transforms *madame's* little shopping car into a 124 mph (200 km/h) road rocket . The engine is fitted into the middle of the car where the back seat should be, and the drive is taken to the back wheels, instead of the front as on the standard Renault 5.

Despite the out-and-out competition looks which make it seem rather out of place on a normal road, the Turbo has few of the vices associated with racers turned street machines.

Off the turbo boost the Turbo can be as docile as a lamb, but give it some throttle and the power comes in with a vengeance. With the driver trying hard, the little car is capable of out-dragging a Lotus Esprit and a Porsche 944 up to 100 mph – beyond that the sheer lack of cubic inches shows up.

Handling is also a Turbo 2 strength. The extended track and the very wide section tires provide more than enough grip to allow this car to hold the road in impressive fashion.

That said, the short overall length of the car means that it responds very promptly to acceleration and braking inputs, and it is certainly fun to drive. But with most of the back taken up by engine, there is no way that there could be room for more than two. Luggage space is negligible, so it's necessary to travel light – but then who needs luggage when you're having fun!

Below: *Wide track and fat tires distinguish Renault's hottest small saloon*

ROLLS-ROYCE SILVER SPIRIT

Whereas the differences between models of cars produced by some manufacturers can be quite startling and obvious, the advances made by Rolls-Royce are harder to spot.

This is never more true than with the latest from the makers of the world's finest automobiles, the Silver Spirit, which features no quantum jump advance, no changes simply for the sake of it, merely a steady advance towards the stated aim of carrying people in such comfort and luxury that they are virtually insulated from the outside world.

The Spirit and the longer wheelbased Spur replace the old Silver Shadow with a new body that is slightly larger than its predecessor's and with a little more interior space. It is perhaps rather less upright than the Shadow, and presents a greater impression of bulk.

Speed is not the name of the game with the Silver Spirit, although the 6.7-liter V8 engine propels this heavy car up to a potential maximum of around 120 mph (193 km/h), and it can reach 60 mph (96.5 km/h) in 10 seconds if pressed. Smooth, steady, and above all silent, progress is the main objective, and the Spirit, like its predecessors, performs to perfection.

The Spirit may be chauffeur-driven, but there is no glass partition between the front and rear compartments, both of which have well-upholstered and comfortable seating finished in a choice of materials – usually hide. The front seats have an electrically operated adjustment.

The standard of the finish is, as might be expected, extremely high. Gallons of paint, painstakingly applied, cover the elegant body panelling, and top class carpeting with matching veneer add to the air of pure elegance.

The Rolls-Royce Silver Spirit is the kind of car that arouses jealousy in the hearts of others, and the famous figure of the Spirit of Ecstasy topping the handsome radiator shell is a magnet for souvenir hunters. But the Spirit has a surprise for anyone meddling with the mascot. One touch activates a powerful spring which swings the lady down into a trapdoor in the top of the shell out of harm's way.

Below: *The Best Car in the World, the Silver Spirit is the latest new car from Rolls-Royce. Interior* (right) *reflects high standards*

SAAB 9000 TURBO 16

The 9000, the new flagship of the range from the Swedish carmaker, is the product of intensive co-operation between Saab and Lancia. The ideal outcome would have been a common car but instead Saab got the 9000 and Lancia the Thema – similar to look at, but very different in detail. In fact, 12 minor body pressings in the engine compartment is all the two cars have completely in common.

For its first new car in 17 years, Saab has broken a few of its established molds. Although retaining front-wheel drive, the powerful twin-cam, 16-valve turbocharged 2-liter engine is fitted transversely, allowing Saab to provide a large amount of interior space. In fact, according to the American EPA (Environmental Protection Agency) index, the 9000 rates with Jaguar, Mercedes and even the Rolls-Royce Silver Spirit when it comes to *lebensraum* (legroom).

The introduction of the 9000 puts Saab into the executive class for the first time – and the high performance executive class at that. The new turbo engine, seen for the first time in the aerodynamic Turbo 16S, endows the car with a top speed of more than 137 mph (220 km/h) and it will hit 60 mph from rest in around eight seconds (0-100 km/h, 8.3 seconds). A 5-speed gearbox is standard, as is power-assisted steering and the provision of large diameter disc brakes all round.

Saab has drawn extensively upon its experience with aircraft to produce the interior styling of the 9000. The design engineers refer to the driving seat as the "cockpit", and one look at the inside shows why. All instrumentation and minor controls are grouped in an L-shaped panel across the dashboard and down into the center console where a clever variable shelf system allows the owner to locate radio and tape equipment, ashtray and lighter or storage box.

Creature comforts feature high on the list of priorities, and those tough Swedish winters mean that Saab know all about keeping people warm in cars. The high power heating and ventilation system is supplemented by thermostatically controlled heating elements in the front seats. Hay fever sufferers benefit from a special filter system in the ventilation unit that traps pollen as well as road dust, soot and oil mist.

Below: *The 9000 is the new flagship for the Saab range. Interior (right) shows aircraft design influence*

TVR 390SE

TVR, the sports car maker based near the seaside resort of Blackpool, has somehow been able to avoid the pitfalls and problems that have afflicted so many of Britain's small specialist car manufacturers.

Perhaps the secret is commitment: TVR build sports cars and nothing else. This philosophy is possibly responsible for the way in which the cars have been received by customers all over Europe and in the USA, a response that has caused TVR to expand in order to cope with demand.

The only problem was that it needed a range leader – a real red-blooded sports car – and so TVR set out to create it. The company had already made substantial improvements to the chassis performance of the old Tasmin convertible and coupé models, so that now the car could handle some more power with ease.

Those earlier cars were powered by a Rover V8 3.5-liter engine to Vitesse specifications. The Rover unit was retained for the new car, but increased in capacity to 3.9 liters. Combined with other modifications, the power output rocketed from the 190 bhp of the standard engine to 275 bhp in its new form. In terms of maximum speed the 390 gains only a modest 10 mph over the 350i model, clocking 144 mph (232 km/h), but it shaves 1.4 seconds from the 0 to 60 mph (96.5 km/h) time and reaches 100 mph (161 km/h) 4.4 seconds sooner than the 350i.

Other changes to the TVR 390SE include fitting a limited slip differential, ventilated front disc brakes for improved stopping power and revised suspension damping. External giveaways on the handsome GRP convertible bodyshell include the big, full-width "chin" spoiler at the front with a balancing spoiler at the rear below the bumper.

Inside refinements include a new instrument panel and re-arranged switchgear, new heating and ventilation systems. Leather trim and real wood veneer for the dashboard and door cappings add to the traditional English sports car feel.

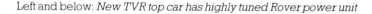

Left and below: *New TVR top car has highly tuned Rover power unit*

VECTOR

One magazine described the Vector as being "like an F16 fighter running around on the ground". Looking at the amazing device produced by Gerry Wiegert it is easy to see how it might be rather more at home in the air that fighting it out at traffic speeds on the road.

In theory, the Vector could achieve maximum speeds of around 200 mph, pushed by Wiegert's modified Chevrolet V8 engine which develops some 600 bhp. In case the Vector driver senses the remote possibility of being out-dragged at the traffic lights, there is a control in the cockpit to boost the power still further.

The similarity to an aircraft is carried through to the chassis, which is made with aluminum box sections and a honeycomb floor all fixed together with aerospace superglue.

There is more of the aeronautical influence inside where the switches, bar graph instruments and seat harnesses are actually taken from an F16 fighter plane – not that those outside will be able to see much because the Vector wears dark glasses – tinted windows keep the driver and passenger private.

The Vector has no standard ignition key, simply a computer-style keypad. Some models cater for the ultimate in in-car entertainment installation, with no less than 24 speakers fitted into the doors to produce the sound from the tape player, CB and radio unit.

Below and left: Vector is like a jetplane on wheels

VOLVO 760 GLE TURBO

Volvo cars are respected for their solidity, longevity and reliability; advantages which compensate for the somewhat stolid styling – the old "Nordic tank" syndrome. With its new flagship, the 760 GLE Turbo, Volvo has tried to break away from this stereotype to produce a stylish and yet imposing saloon, able to hold its own in executive company.

The design has clearly been influenced by American ideas, especially towards the rear with the steeply raked, sharp-cut rear window treatment and the addition of the small rear quarter light.

Although the overall length is no longer than that of the 240 saloon, the 760 sits on a longer wheelbase and offers much more interior space, and the square tail houses a capacious trunk area.

There is a wide variety of engine options, including a 2.8-liter version of the V6 jointly developed with Peugeot and Renault and a 6-cylinder turbo diesel.

Even so, the 760 – being a heavy car – requires even more urge if it is to earn itself a place in the executive express league, so the petrol engine turbo is a worthwhile consideration and gives the car a maximum speed potential of 125 mph (201 km/h).

Volvo has deliberately chosen a small turbo to harness to the 2.3-liter 4-cylinder engine in order to control the boost. Now with an electronic engine management system, the power delivery can be smoothed without the usual turbo lag. The standard gearbox is a 4-speed manual with an electrically engaged overdrive fifth gear.

The luxury interior of the car features soft leather upholstery, and the seats in front have heated elements in the cushions that come on automatically whenever the temperature falls below a certain level. As might be expected from a car made where cold conditions are well known, the heater system – which includes integrated air conditioning – keeps the occupants comfortable.

Below and following page: Stylish big car from Sweden. Lots of space and the turbo adds the pace

PICTURE CREDITS

A.A. Picture Library 24 **Audi** 17 **Autocar** 80, Andrew Yeadon contents spread, 16, 78-79, 91 **Bertone** 56 bottom, 57 bottom, 69 **Neill Bruce** 50, 51 **BMW** 23, 25
Cadillac 28-29, 30-31 **Chrysler/Plymouth** 36-37, 37, 38-39, 40, 41 **Daimler-Benz** 74-75 **Mirco Decet** 68 inset **Excalibur Motor Corporation** title page, 48-49 **Ferrari**
52-53, 54-55 **Focalpoint/Lancia** 70 top, **Focalpoint/Lotus Cars** 6 **Ford Motor Company** 58-63 all pictures **General Motors** 8-9 **Hurlston Design** 64-65, 66-67, 67
L.A.T. Photographic 18-19 **Lancia** 70 bottom **O.A. Maserati Auto** 44-45, 72-73 **Mitsubishi** 77 inset, Maynard Adams 76-77 **Andrew Morland** 45, 92, 92-93
Multimedia Bob Hill 34, 35, Andrew Morland 22, 42-43, Nicky Wright 32-33 **National Motor Museum, Beaulieu** half title page, 46, 47, 70-71 **Outline Creative/Aston
Martin** 10-11, 12, 13, 14-15 **The Photosource** front cover **Porsche** 82-83, 84 bottom **Quadrant Picture Library** 26-27, 68, 73, 85 **Peter Roberts** 21 bottom, 56-57, back
cover **Rolls-Royce Motors** 9, 20-21, 21 top, 86-87, 87 inset **Saab GB Ltd.** 88-89 **Saab-Scania** 89 inset **Sloniger** 81, 84 **TVR** 90-91 **Volvo Car Corporation** 94-95, 96

Multimedia Publications (UK) Limited has endeavored to observe the legal requirements with regard to the rights of suppliers of photographic material.